MAMMALS

BookLife
PUBLISHING

©2019
BookLife Publishing Ltd.
King's Lynn
Norfolk PE30 4LS

ISBN: 978-1-78637-672-5

Written by:
Joanna Brundle

Edited by:
John Wood

Designed by:
Dan Scase

All facts, statistics, web addresses
and URLs in this book were verified
as valid and accurate at time of
writing. No responsibility for any
changes to external websites or
references can be accepted by
either the author or publisher.

PHOTO CREDITS

All images are courtesy of Shutterstock.com, unless otherwise specified. With thanks to Getty Images, Thinkstock Photo and iStockphoto. Front Cover – Kris Wiktor. 2 – Kris Wiktor. 4 – Monkey Business Images, michael sheehan. 5 – Syda Productions, ChWeiss. 6 – Eric Gevaert, FloridaStock. 7 – Menno Schaefer, frank60. 8 – Yann hubert, Andrzej Kubik. 9 – Jez Bennett, Hit1912. 10 – Menno Schaefer, reisegraf.ch. 11 – MZPHOTO.CZ. 12 – Steve Cymro, Christopher Gardiner. 13 – vkilikov, erichon. 14 – Michal Pesata, Breck P. Kent. 15 – Alizada Studios, Alexius Sutandio. 16 – worldswildlifewonders, Wayne Butterworth. 17 – Jarrod Calati. 18 – Rob kemp, GUDKOV ANDREY. 19 – Kjersti Joergensen, Kritskiy-ua. 20 – Stowen Seto, Budimir Jevtic. 21 – Marek Velechovsky, Bildagentur Zoonar GmbH. 22 – anetapics, Susan Flashman. 23 – Tracey Essery, EcoPrint. 24 – Hans Wagemaker, Adalbert Dragon. 25 – belizar, Kris Wiktor. 26 – GUDKOV ANDREY, Karen Hadley. 27 – Krista Kennell, PicksArt. 28 – Eugene Troskie, Aleksandr Kutskii. 29 – William Healy Photography, Jimmy Viana. 30 – Osadchaya Olga, topdigipro, The Dog Photographer, mcherevan. Cheetah vectors throughout – Sketch Master. Jungle vector throughout – Ammak, SaveJungle. Background – Only background.

CONTENTS

PAGE 4   What Is Reproduction?
PAGE 6   What Are Mammals?
PAGE 8   Courtship and Mating
PAGE 10   Territories
PAGE 12   Placental Mammals
PAGE 14   Pouched Mammals
PAGE 16   Monotremes
PAGE 18   Mammal Young
PAGE 20   Mammal Parents
PAGE 22   Reproduction in Meerkats
PAGE 24   Reproduction in Jaguars
PAGE 26   Mammals Under Threat
PAGE 28   Fascinating Facts
PAGE 31   Glossary
PAGE 32   Index

Words that look like THIS can be found in the glossary on page 31.

WHAT IS REPRODUCTION?

These grandparents and parents have reproduced to give birth to new GENERATIONS.

Have you ever wondered how you and all the other animals and plants in our world came to be here? Where did we all come from? These are big questions, but the answer is simple – reproduction. Reproduction is the process by which all living things make more of themselves. It is common to all living things, from the blue whale, the largest animal on Earth, to the tiniest living things that can only be seen under a microscope. Mammals, birds, fish, reptiles, amphibians, insects and plants all need to reproduce. You are here because your parents have reproduced, as their parents did before them.

WHY IS REPRODUCTION IMPORTANT?

Reproduction is important because all living things have a LIFESPAN and will eventually die. They must therefore reproduce to make sure that their SPECIES continues and does not die out. This is sometimes called the 'circle of life'.

African bush elephant with her calf

THE EARLIEST MAMMALS WERE TINY, MOUSE-LIKE CREATURES THAT LIVED AROUND 210 MILLION YEARS AGO.

Let's have some cubs of our own.

Yes, we don't want our species to become EXTINCT.

4

SEXUAL AND ASEXUAL REPRODUCTION

Sexual reproduction requires one male and one female parent. New life is made by putting together genetic information (instructions about how growth and development take place) from the two parents. Genetic information is found inside <u>CELLS</u>, including sex cells called gametes. In males, gametes are called sperm. In females, gametes are called eggs. During sexual reproduction, the two gametes join together. This process is called fertilisation. When an egg and sperm cell join, they form a fertilised egg. This then begins to divide again and again to form an <u>EMBRYO</u>. The embryo grows to become a new lifeform that carries similar genetic information to both parents but is not exactly the same as either.

The members of this family look similar to one another. They share genetic information but are not exactly the same.

WHEN YOUNG THAT ARE PRODUCED BY ASEXUAL REPRODUCTION HAVE GENETIC INFORMATION WHICH IS EXACTLY THE SAME AS THAT OF THEIR PARENT, THEY ARE CALLED CLONES.

Asexual reproduction requires one parent. The young that are produced carry exactly the same genetic information as the parent. Asexual reproduction may take place as a result of a process called parthenogenesis (say: par-thu-no-jen-u-sis), in which eggs develop into embryos without having been fertilised by sperm. Budding, <u>FRAGMENTATION</u> and <u>FISSION</u> are other common forms of asexual reproduction. Asexual reproduction is very rare in animals but is commonly seen in <u>BACTERIA</u>, fungi and plants.

Plantlets

Budding is a form of asexual reproduction in plants. Plantlets grow from the parent plant before detaching and continuing to grow on their own.

There are words there that I've never seen before.

Let's look at page 31 to help us.

WHAT ARE MAMMALS?

The animal kingdom is divided into smaller groups called phyla. Each phylum groups together animals that are alike in important ways. Along with reptiles, amphibians, fish and birds, mammals are vertebrates. This means they have a backbone. Each phylum is split into smaller groups called classes. Mammals belong to the class called Mammalia. Like birds, mammals are warm-blooded. This means that they can control their body temperature, whatever the temperature of their environment. Mammals are found on every continent and in every ocean. They are ADAPTED to live in every type of HABITAT, from tropical rainforests to sea ice. They come in all sorts of sizes, from the tiny bumblebee bat, which is only about three centimetres (cm) long, to the blue whale, which may be up to 30 metres (m) long. Almost all mammals are viviparous, meaning that they give birth to live young. All mammals reproduce sexually, but their young develop in different ways. Take a look at pages 12 to 17 to find out more.

Rainforests are home to many different mammals including lemurs, bats, monkeys, leopards and jaguars.

SCIENTISTS THINK THAT THERE ARE AROUND 5,500 SPECIES OF MAMMAL ALIVE TODAY.

Polar bears live and breed on Arctic sea ice.

WHAT DO ALL MAMMALS HAVE IN COMMON?

Mammals have particular things in common. These make them different from other classes of vertebrates.

Nearly all mammals have fur or hair of some sort. This keeps them warm and helps to protect them from injury. Mammals that live in hot places or in the sea have very fine hair or hair that is only there at birth. In porcupines and hedgehogs, hairs have become spines, used for defence.

Sea otters are one of the hairiest mammals. Their thick fur keeps them warm and traps air, helping them to float.

All young mammals are <u>NOURISHED</u> by milk from their mothers. The milk is produced in <u>MAMMARY GLANDS</u>, which give mammals their name. Mammary glands are found on either side of the mother's chest, in her groin or on her belly. Drinking milk from the mother's teats is called suckling.

These puppies are suckling.

COURTSHIP AND MATING

Different species attract mates in different ways, using mating calls, smells and signals. Some males fight with other males for an area that they control, called their <u>TERRITORY</u>.

SINGING

Male mice try to impress a female by singing. These 'songs' are so high pitched that humans cannot hear them. When the sounds are recorded and slowed down so that we can hear them, they sound like the songs that birds use to attract a mate. Mammals that live in the huge oceans have to find a mate who may be far away. They use singing to do this because sound travels a long way under water. Humpback whales sing particularly beautifully, putting together many different sounds, from roars to squeals.

During the mating season, humpback whales <u>MIGRATE</u> from icy, polar seas to warm, tropical seas to breed.

FIGHTING

During the mating season, male giraffes may fight one another for the right to mate with females in the area. They take it in turns to use their powerful necks to crash into their opponent. These battles may lead to serious injury, or even death, for the loser.

YOUNG MALES OFTEN HAVE DISPLAY FIGHTS. THESE ARE NOT REAL FIGHTS – THE GIRAFFES ARE TESTING ONE ANOTHER'S STRENGTH.

Giraffes fighting, or 'necking'

SCENTS AND SIGNALS

This male lion is scenting by urinating (weeing) to mark his territory.

Some mammals produce special scents to mark their territory and warn off other males. At certain times of the year, when food will be plentiful at the time the young will be born, most female mammals will release pheromones. A pheromone is something that is detected by other members of the species, and it shows that an animal is ready to mate. Among many species of mammal, the male is larger and has particular markings. The male mandrill, for example, is over twice the size of the female. He is also much more colourful, with purple, blue and red skin on his bottom and face. The brighter his colours, the more likely he is to mate. He warns off other males by strutting and by standing in a threatening pose.

Male mandrill

Usually, the male climbs onto the female's back to mate. Fertilisation takes place inside her body. Most mammal species mate with different partners through their lives. Beavers, wolves and otters are some of the few mammal species that choose one mate for life.

TERRITORIES

Many mammals have a territory that they defend against other members of their species. The territory is a place to find food and a partner, and to mate. It also provides a safe place for young to be born and raised.

The time when male deer fight for females is called the rutting season.

LEKS

Some mammals, such as fallow deer and kob antelopes, set up a territory called a lek for the mating season. The lek is like a stage, where the males show off to the females by fighting with other males. They fight by pushing and shoving and locking antlers or horns. The females watch the displays and choose a mate based on his strength and success.

CALLING

Wolves mark their territory by howling. All the members of the wolf pack howl together to warn off other packs and to show that the territory is well defended. Howler monkeys live in small groups of one or two males and several females. The male has one of the loudest calls of any land mammal, which he uses to warn other males to stay away.

DEFENDING A TERRITORY TAKES TIME AND LOTS OF ENERGY, SO SOME MAMMALS ONLY DEFEND A TERRITORY DURING THE MATING SEASON.

The calls of howler monkeys can travel several kilometres through the rainforest.

BEACH TERRITORIES

The male elephant seal takes its name from its trunk-like snout, which it uses to make loud roars that scare other males away.

Unlike dolphins and whales that spend their whole lives in the ocean, some marine mammals, such as elephant seals, come ashore to mate and to give birth. They usually head for quiet beaches. Each male fights for his own territory on the beach, which he then fiercely defends against any other males. Males threaten other males by rising up on their front flippers. They also call loudly and lunge at one another. The females usually come ashore once the territories have been won. They are already pregnant with pups from the previous mating season. After giving birth, they mate again.

HIPPOS

The male hippopotamus is one of the most fiercely territorial mammals. His territory contains the females he has mated with, as well as their young. When two males challenge one another, they open their huge mouths as wide as they can to show off their teeth and long, sharp tusks. If neither male gives in, they fight. The loser may get seriously injured or even die.

IF A HIPPO CALF IS CAUGHT IN THE FIGHTING, IT CAN BE SERIOUSLY HURT OR CRUSHED.

PLACENTAL MAMMALS

Mammals fall into one of three groups, depending on how their young develop. By far the largest group is the placental mammals, also known as eutheria (say: you-thear-ree-a). A fertilised egg attaches to the wall of an ORGAN inside the mother, called her UTERUS, or womb. The young then develop inside the uterus. The young of placental mammals are well developed at birth, compared to the young of other mammal groups.

THE PLACENTA

The placenta is a TEMPORARY organ in pregnant placental mammals. It is rich in blood and is fixed into the wall of the uterus. The placenta acts as an exchange between the mother and her young. Nutrients and OXYGEN pass from the mother to the young. Waste products pass the other way. The umbilical cord links the placenta to the young.

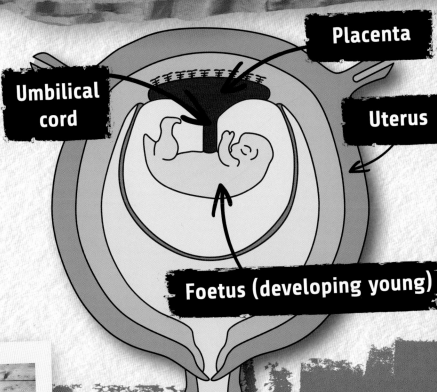

Placenta

Umbilical cord

Uterus

Foetus (developing young)

GESTATION

The larger the animal, the longer the gestation period and the fewer young in a LITTER. Hamsters give birth to around eight young after 15 days. Rhinos give birth after about 450 days, usually to just one calf. The time when the young are developing before birth is called the gestation period.

Horses usually give birth to a single foal after a gestation period of 11 to 12 months.

GIVING BIRTH

Placental mammals give birth in several different ways. An elephant gives birth directly onto the ground, surrounded by other females in her herd. They may help the mother by gently pushing the calf onto its feet. Polar bears dig into deep snow drifts to make cosy nests that protect their young from wind and cold. Seal pups may be born onto ice. Dolphins, whales, dugongs and manatees give birth under water.

A dolphin calf is born tail first to stop it from drowning. It is pushed by the mother to the surface to take its first breath.

DEVELOPMENT AT BIRTH

Some newborn placental mammals, although well developed, have no fur and cannot see, hear or stand. They need their mother for survival. Those with a longer gestation period are usually born with a protective coating of hair or fur. They can see and hear, and they can usually swim straightaway or stand soon after birth. Within a few minutes of birth, newborn wildebeest can run fast enough to keep up with their herd. This helps to protect them from PREDATORS.

Wildebeest are born after a gestation period of around 257 days.

FOALS CAN GALLOP JUST 24 HOURS AFTER BIRTH.

13

POUCHED MAMMALS

Pouched mammals are the second-largest group of mammals. They are also known as marsupials (say: mar-soop-ee-als).

A pouched mammal also begins life as a fertilised egg in the mother's uterus, but it spends very little time developing there. It is born before it is fully formed and is hairless and blind. Although it seems helpless, its front legs are developed enough to allow it to crawl from the birth opening to a pouch on the mother's belly. It does this by INSTINCT and uses its senses of smell and touch to find its way. The mother helps by licking a pathway through her fur to guide the baby. Marsupial young are known as joeys. Once a joey has found its way inside the pouch, it feeds by latching on to one of the mother's NIPPLES. The nipple then swells so that the joey cannot let go until it is fully formed. The inside of the pouch is usually hairless, but the mother's skin provides warmth.

Pouched mammals include wallabies, koalas, kangaroos, wombats, possums and opossums.

A MARSUPIAL MOTHER KEEPS THE INSIDE OF HER POUCH CLEAN BY USING HER TONGUE TO REMOVE WASTE FROM THE YOUNG.

Baby opossums in the mother's pouch

Oh dear. I haven't got a pouch.

That's because we're not pouched mammals.

GROWING UP

A koala joey ventures out of the pouch after six months, but stays close to the mother, often riding on her back.

The mother's milk contains lots of nutrients, and a joey grows quickly. Its ears and eyes open and fur begins to appear. When it is well developed and looks like a small adult, it takes a first peek outside the pouch. The mother gently tips it out of the pouch and it begins to move about on its own. As the joey grows, it spends more and more time outside the pouch, but it hops straight back in if there is any danger. Some pouched mammals continue to suckle on their mother's nipple, even after they are too big to fit in the pouch. Grey kangaroos, for example, leave the pouch after 11 months but may continue to suckle until they are 18 months old.

QUICK WORK

The eastern barred bandicoot is one of the fastest mammal breeders. The young are usually born after just 11 days in the uterus. They then spend about 55 days in the pouch. The young stay close to the mother for a week or two after leaving the pouch.

Eastern barred bandicoots reach sexual maturity (the age at which they can reproduce) at just three months old.

MONOTREMES

Monotremes are the smallest group of mammals by far, and the most unusual. Unlike all other mammals, monotremes are oviparous. This means that they lay eggs, rather than giving birth to live young. They have a single body opening, called a cloaca, for getting rid of waste. Females also use the cloaca for reproduction. In these ways, monotremes seem similar to reptiles, but they are classed as mammals because they have fur or spines and produce milk for their young.

Duck-billed platypus

Platypuses may lay up to three eggs. Echidnas lay just one egg.

MATING AND EGG-LAYING

Short-nosed echidna

Echidnas are also known as spiny anteaters.

Monotremes live on their own and only come together to mate. Fertilisation takes place inside the mother's body, where the young develop for 12 to 21 days. A soft, leathery shell develops before the egg is laid. During the mating season, a pouch-like fold develops on the belly of the female echidna. After laying her egg, she rolls it down her tummy into the fold, where it is <u>INCUBATED</u> by warmth from her body. The female platypus lays her eggs in her burrow. She curls her body around them to protect them and keep them warm.

GROWING UP

After about ten days, the young hatch. A young echidna, known as a puggle, stays in the pouch for two to three months until its spines begin to harden. It laps milk from special PORES on the mother's belly. Once the puggle has left the pouch, it may stay in a burrow dug by the mother for up to seven months. She leaves the puggle in the safety of the burrow while she goes out to look for food. The mother platypus incubates her eggs by using her tail to press them against her warm body. Like echidnas, the platypus has no teats for the young to suck. Milk is released through two patches in the mother's skin and collects in grooves on her belly. The young stay in the burrow for about four months. After this time, they are ready to leave the burrow and learn to swim and find food for themselves.

Echidnas have large, clawed feet for digging their burrows.

MONOTREMES DEVELOP A SHARP GROWTH CALLED AN EGG TOOTH, WHICH THEY USE TO BREAK OUT OF THEIR SOFT SHELL. AFTER A FEW DAYS, THE EGG TOOTH FALLS OFF.

MAMMAL YOUNG

All placental and marsupial mammal young know by instinct how to suck milk from the mother's teats. A few minutes after birth, for example, a dolphin calf dives underneath its mother's body and latches on to one of her teats. A young mammal may push against the mother's udder to start the flow of milk.

Hungry lambs appear to head-butt their mother's udder.

WEANING

Mammal young slowly begin to eat solid food. At first, they continue to suckle as well. Replacing the mother's milk with solid food is called weaning. Some young mammals that live in packs, such as wild dogs, lick the face of an adult to beg for food. The adult then <u>REGURGITATES</u> chewed up meat to feed them.

LEARNING

Young mammals spend lots of time playing with other youngsters. Play-fights make them strong, while gentle biting and nipping teaches them how sharp their teeth are. The cubs of large cats, such as cheetahs, wrestle with one another, trying out their claws and teeth. This prepares them for when they have to hunt for <u>PREY</u> themselves.

Cheetah cubs playing

A river otter is taught all the skills it needs to survive by its mother.

Species that hunt must be able to STALK their prey silently, run quickly and pounce at the right moment. Young mammals learn these skills by watching, copying and practising. Elephant calves watch the adults in their herd to learn which plants to eat and how to use their trunks. Newborn river otters are blind and helpless and have to be taught how to swim and dive under the water by their mother. She also shows the pups how to catch fish. Sometimes, she brings half-dead fish she has caught back to the pups, so that they can try out their hunting skills close to the river bank.

LIVING ALONE

Rodents and other small mammals begin to live on their own almost as soon as they finish suckling. They survive using instinctive behaviour, rather than by copying or learning. The young of larger mammals may stay with their mothers for several years. Young PRIMATES take longer to grow up and start looking after themselves than any other mammals.

Squirrels do not stay with their mothers long enough to learn how to find and bury nuts and run up trees. Their behaviour is instinctive.

SCORPIONS ARE AN IMPORTANT FOOD FOR MEERKATS. MEERKAT PUPS HAVE TO BE TAUGHT HOW TO BITE OFF THE SCORPION'S STINGING TAIL BEFORE EATING THE REST.

19

MAMMAL PARENTS

Most mammal mothers take great care of their young. In some cases, this care carries on for years. During this time, the young continue to learn from the mother. In most mammal species, the mother cares for the young on her own.

NURSING

The mother's milk contains all the nutrients that the young need. It also contains antibodies. These give the young protection against diseases. The nursing period – the time for which the young drink the mother's milk – is different for different species. Rhinos, elephants and other large mammals nurse their young for several years, whereas hooded seals nurse their pups for only four days.

Orangutans nurse their young for seven years, one of the longest nursing periods of any mammal.

LOVING CARE

MOTHER PIGS SING TO THEIR PIGLETS WHILE NURSING THEM – JUST LIKE HUMAN MOTHERS DO! BABY PIGS CAN RECOGNISE THEIR MOTHER'S VOICE, AND CAN RESPOND TO THEIR OWN NAMES WHEN SHE CALLS THEM.

The mother may feed her young standing up or lying down.

In most monkey and ape species, the mother has a very strong bond with her baby. She carries the baby around with her on her belly or back as she swings through the trees. Elephant mothers use their trunks to stroke and encourage their calf. On the move, the rest of the herd slows down if the calf cannot keep up.

MALE PARENTS

Care of the young by mammal fathers is very rare, but it is seen in a few species, including wolves and marmosets. Male marmosets take care of their newborn young by licking and grooming them at birth. Male foxes also look after their young while the female is out finding food.

FAMILY GROUPS

The male bat-eared fox spends as much time guarding and raising his young as the female.

Some mammals, such as lions and elephants, are raised in family groups of females and their young. Others, such as zebra and deer, live in large herds. This gives some protection from predators. Wolves live in a pack. Each pack has a strict order of importance called a hierarchy (say: high-uh-rah-kee). Only the most important male and female, known as the alpha pair, are allowed to breed. The alpha female has a litter of up to seven pups that are cared for by both the mother and father. The other pack members all help to care for the cubs too. By doing this, they learn important lessons about looking after young that will help them when they leave to begin their own pack.

Wolf cubs with their mother

REPRODUCTION IN MEERKATS

Meerkats are small carnivores (meat eaters) that live in groups in desert habitats across Africa. Each group of up to 50 animals has an alpha pair, to whom most of the other members are related. The alpha female is usually the largest female in the group and only the alpha female is allowed to reproduce. If any other female becomes pregnant, she will remove her from the burrow and may even kill her pups. Both males and females reach sexual maturity by the age of one year.

Meerkats are placental mammals that live in groups, called gangs or mobs.

GESTATION AND BIRTH

Meerkat gangs dig several underground burrows, each with a grass-lined space at the end of a series of tunnels. The female gives birth at night in one of these burrows, where the pups are safe from predators, such as jackals and eagles. Most litters have three pups, which are born after a gestation period of 70 days. Pups are born blind, deaf and with very little fur. They stay hidden in the burrow with their mother for two to three weeks.

Meerkat pups suckle from teats on the mother's belly.

SHARED CARE

The meerkats in each gang work together to care for the pups. The pups are weaned after about two months and are left with a 'babysitter' when the mother and other gang members go hunting. The hunters feed whoever is closest when they return, so the pups quickly learn to fight for food. Gang members of both sexes take it in turns to guard the burrow, feed the pups and act as lookouts while the rest of the group is hunting.

The lookout climbs to a high place and stands on its hind legs to get the best view of any approaching predators.

IF THE LOOKOUT SPOTS A PREDATOR, IT GIVES A WARNING CRY AND THE WHOLE GANG RUNS TO SAFETY.

GROWING UP

Meerkat pups play-fighting

Young pups have squeaky, high-pitched cries that tell the adults they are hungry. As they get older, their cries become lower in pitch and the adults take less notice. This encourages the pups to start fending for themselves. Pups play-fight to learn and practise hunting skills. They also learn how to take part in fierce battles for territory against neighbouring gangs. Some leave their gang after a year or so, to begin gangs of their own. Others stay all their lives, helping the alpha pair to care for new litters.

23

REPRODUCTION IN JAGUARS

Unlike other members of the cat family, jaguars love the water and swim, play and hunt in streams and pools.

Jaguars are found in South and Central America and, very rarely, in southern states of the US. They are good swimmers and climbers and live in swamps or forests, where thick plant cover helps them to stalk their prey.

Jaguars normally live and hunt on their own, only coming together to mate. The male reaches sexual maturity (the age at which he is ready to reproduce) at around three to four years of age. For females, it is younger – normally around two years of age. When the female comes into her special breeding time, she scents by leaving strong-smelling urine (wee) on trees. The smell tells male jaguars that she is ready to mate. She also has special calls that help the males to find her. Males will fight for the right to mate with her. They also fiercely defend their territory and any females living in it against other males. Mating prompts the female's body to produce eggs, which are fertilised inside her body with sperm from the male.

Jaguars have sharp teeth and powerful jaws. They kill their prey with a single bite to the skull.

I'm four years old and you're two.

So maybe it's time to add one more?

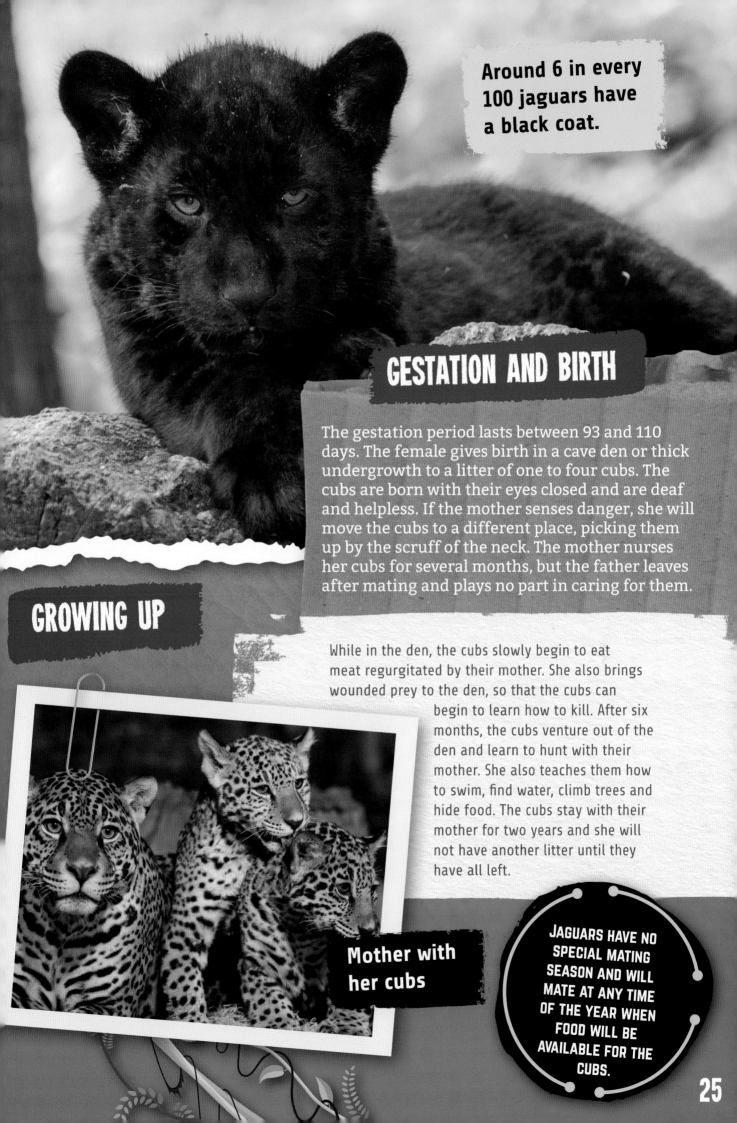

Around 6 in every 100 jaguars have a black coat.

GESTATION AND BIRTH

The gestation period lasts between 93 and 110 days. The female gives birth in a cave den or thick undergrowth to a litter of one to four cubs. The cubs are born with their eyes closed and are deaf and helpless. If the mother senses danger, she will move the cubs to a different place, picking them up by the scruff of the neck. The mother nurses her cubs for several months, but the father leaves after mating and plays no part in caring for them.

GROWING UP

While in the den, the cubs slowly begin to eat meat regurgitated by their mother. She also brings wounded prey to the den, so that the cubs can begin to learn how to kill. After six months, the cubs venture out of the den and learn to hunt with their mother. She also teaches them how to swim, find water, climb trees and hide food. The cubs stay with their mother for two years and she will not have another litter until they have all left.

Mother with her cubs

JAGUARS HAVE NO SPECIAL MATING SEASON AND WILL MATE AT ANY TIME OF THE YEAR WHEN FOOD WILL BE AVAILABLE FOR THE CUBS.

MAMMALS UNDER THREAT

Mountain gorillas are critically endangered due to loss of habitat, hunting and war.

The IUCN (International Union for the Conservation of Nature) puts together a list called the Red List. This ranks endangered plants and animals in one of five groups, from 'least concern' to 'CRITICALLY ENDANGERED'. According to the Red List, one-quarter of all mammal species are threatened with extinction. This problem has been caused by human activities, including hunting, habitat destruction (particularly DEFORESTATION) and GLOBAL WARMING. Sumatran orangutans are classed as critically endangered. Their greatest threat is deforestation of their rainforest habitats to make way for housing, farming, mining, roads and tourism. White rhinos have been brought to the edge of extinction by hunters. Rhino horns are valuable as they are used in traditional medicines and are also a sign of wealth in some cultures. More than 7,000 rhinos were killed in South Africa alone between 2008 and 2018. Conservationists – people who care about protecting the environment – are removing rhinos' horns, so that hunters will leave them alone. The animals are SEDATED using a dart and the horns are then sawn off by a vet.

Are we on the Red List?

Yes, our numbers are going down and we're classed as 'near threatened'. That means we could be threatened with extinction in the future.

Whereas hunters kill the rhino to remove their horns, this animal's horns have been painlessly removed by a vet.

DAME JANE MORRIS GOODALL

Dame Jane Morris Goodall is a conservationist and expert on chimpanzees. She has encouraged people to think about conservation in a different way that looks at the needs of local people, as well as the environment. The worldwide conservation group that she began, called The Jane Goodall Institute, works to protect chimpanzees and to encourage people to look after the natural world. Today, she speaks to people around the world about threats to chimpanzees and about environmental problems. She urges people to take action on behalf of all living things that share our planet.

Dame Jane Goodall spent 55 years studying the lives of chimpanzees.

SUCCESS STORIES

Some species, such as the black rhinoceros and grey whale, have been rescued from the edge of extinction. This has happened thanks to protection of their habitats and control of hunting. Programmes that allow animals to breed safely in zoos and wildlife SANCTUARIES have also helped. Nature-based travel, known as ecotourism, is becoming popular. It allows tourists to view nature in a way that does not harm animals or their breeding grounds. The money that is made is used for conservation programmes.

Deforestation drove the golden lion tamarind from its Brazilian rainforest habitat, but sanctuaries have been set up to protect this species and numbers are rising.

FASCINATING FACTS

MUSK OXEN

Musk oxen live in the Arctic in herds of up to 30 animals. They are normally very peaceful animals. If predators such as Arctic wolves and dogs threaten them, however, all the adults make a circle around their young. They all face outwards, ready to charge using their sharp horns. The horns of the male may be up to 60 cm long and form a band that crosses his forehead. In the mating – or rutting – season, males charge one another head-on to fight for the right to mate with the females in the herd. The noise of the collision can be heard up to a kilometre away.

PANGOLINS

Pangolins are one of the most unusual placental mammals. Rather than fur or hair, they have overlapping scales covering their bodies. The scales protect them from predators. Pangolin young are born with soft scales, but after a few weeks, the scales harden to form a protective layer. Two of the eight species of pangolin are critically endangered.

The pangolin looks like a pine cone with a head, tail and legs.

A wombat joey would quickly suffocate in sand if the mother's pouch did not face backwards. The joey stays inside the pouch for about five months.

PERFECT POUCHES

Wombats and marsupial moles live in sandy desert habitats in Australia. They burrow through sand using their powerful front claws. Rather than facing forwards, the mother's pouch faces backwards. This protects the young from being splattered with loose sand as the mother digs. A koala's pouch opens towards her back legs. She cannot reach into the pouch to clean it but has a clever solution to this problem. Before giving birth, she produces a special germ-killing fluid which goes into the pouch, so that it is germ-free for the arrival of her young. Kangaroos use their tongues to lick their pouches clean before the young climb in.

The short-tailed opossum has one of the shortest gestation periods of any mammal. Around ten young are born after about two weeks.

Although most marsupials have a pouch or temporary fold of skin, some opossum species, such as the short-tailed opossum, have no pouch at all. The mother's teats are on her belly and the newborn young attach firmly to these teats at first. Later on, the young are carried on the mother's back, using their tails and claws to cling on.

OH, RATS!

Parts of India are covered with a type of bamboo that only flowers once every 48 years. The plant produces fruit and huge amounts of seed before dying off. Millions of rats are attracted to this food. Rats can have a litter of babies every three weeks and these young can then reproduce by the age of 50 to 60 days. The plentiful food supply means that the rats reproduce successfully. They have larger litters than normal and fewer young die. After eating all the bamboo seed, the huge numbers of rats then destroy growing crops. This is an example of how environmental factors can affect reproduction.

CROSS-BREEDING

We have seen that sexual reproduction produces young that carry genetic information from both parents. If a male and female from different species mate, the young have characteristics of both species. A liger, for example, is the young of a male lion and a female tiger and is similar to both. Dog breeders sometimes mate two different types of dog to produce a new types, called a cross-breed.

Labradoodle

A labradoodle is a labrador cross-bred with a poodle. In what ways is the labradoodle similar to each of these species?

Poodle

Labrador

Liger

GLOSSARY

ADAPTED changed over time to suit different conditions

BACTERIA tiny, single-celled organisms

CELLS the basic units that make up all living things

CRITICALLY ENDANGERED threatened to the point of becoming almost extinct

DEFORESTATION the cutting down and removal of trees in a forest

EMBRYO an unborn or unhatched young in the process of development

EXTINCT completely died out so that no living representatives of a species remain

FISSION a form of asexual reproduction in which the parent cells of an organism divide to make new cells that are exactly the same as the parent cells

FRAGMENTATION a form of asexual reproduction in which an organism splits into fragments, each of which becomes a new individual that is exactly the same as the parent

GENERATIONS groups of animals of the same species that are roughly the same age

GLOBAL WARMING the gradual rise in the Earth's temperature, caused by the burning of coal, oil and gas

HABITAT the natural environment in which animals or plants live

INCUBATED kept warm to bring about hatching

INSTINCT a pattern of natural behaviour that is inborn and has not been learnt

LIFESPAN the period of time for which a person, animal or plant lives or is expected to live

LITTER a group of young born at the same time

MAMMARY GLANDS organs found in the body of a female mammal, that produce milk for young

MIGRATE move from one habitat or region to another when the seasons change, for food or to mate and rear young

NIPPLES raised parts at the centre of the mammary glands, through which milk passes

NOURISHED supplied with food and everything needed for healthy development

ORGAN a part of the body, such as the heart or liver, that has a particular function

OXYGEN a colourless gas found in air and dissolved in water that is essential for life

PORES tiny openings in the surface of the skin through which gases and liquids can pass

PREDATORS animals that hunt other animals for food

PREY animals that are hunted by other animals for food

PRIMATES members of an order of mammals that includes apes, monkeys and humans

REGURGITATES brings swallowed food up again into the mouth

SANCTUARIES places, usually a piece of land, that are used as protection and shelter for wild animals

SEDATED brought to a state of being asleep or very relaxed by the use of a medicine called a sedative

SPECIES a group of very similar animals or plants that can produce young together

STALK approach quietly and secretly, without attracting attention

TEMPORARY lasting only for a short time

TERRITORY an area defended by an animal or animals against others of the same species

UTERUS an organ inside the female body for containing and nourishing young before they are born

INDEX

A

alpha pair 21–23
antibodies 20

B

burrows 16–17, 22–23, 29

C

cells 5
cloacas 16
clones 5
conservation 26–27

D

deforestation 26–27

E

ecotourism 27
egg teeth 17
eggs 5, 12, 14, 16–17, 24
embryos 5
extinction 4, 26–27

F

fertilisation 5, 9, 16
fur 7, 13–16, 22, 28

G

gametes 5
gestation periods 12–13, 22, 25, 29
global warming 26
Goodall, Dame Jane 27

H

habitats 6, 22, 26–27, 29
hair 7, 13–14, 28
herds 13, 19–21, 28
hierarchy 21
hunting 18–19, 23–27

I

incubation 16–17
instinct 14, 18–19
IUCN (International Union for the Conservation of Nature) 26

J

joeys 14–15, 29

L

leks 10

M

mammary glands 7
mating 8–11, 16, 24–25, 28, 30
migration 8
milk 7, 15–18, 20

N

nursing periods 20

O

oceans 6, 8, 11
oviparous mammals 16

P

parthenogenesis 5
pheromones 9
placental mammals 12–13, 18, 22, 28
placentas 12
pouched mammals 14–17, 29
predators 13, 21–23, 28
prey 18–19, 24–25

R

rainforests 6, 10, 26–27
Red List 26
reproduction
– asexual 5
– sexual 5–6, 30
rutting season 10

S

scenting 9
sexual maturity (age of) 15, 22, 24
solid food 18
sperm 5, 24
suckling 7, 19

T

teats 7, 17–18, 22, 29
territories 8–11, 23–24

U

udders 18
umbilical cords 12
uteruses 12, 14–15

V

viviparous mammals 6

W

weaning 18, 23